SCHOLASTIC

Shapes & Patterns

PLUS

S0-CWT-688

- Sorting
- Classifying
- Measuring
- Counting

by Ellen Booth Church

Printed in the U.S.A.
ISBN 0-590-97702-4
1 2 3 4 5 6 7 8 9 10   02 01 00 99 98 97 96

Scholastic Inc.
New York Toronto London Auckland Sydney

A Message to Parents

Welcome to the fun!

Dear Parents,

The foundation stages of math learning are very visual and observational. When your child identifies shapes, patterns, sizes, and commonalities, he or she uses essential math thinking skills that support all future number work. At the same time, your child is developing important mathematical vocabulary: *same, different, big, bigger, biggest, small, smaller, smallest, more, less, equal.*

Shapes and Patterns provides fun and practice with essential math skills. The activities are organized by concept: *sorting and classifying, patterns, shapes,* and *measuring and comparing.* Each section provides a range of skill levels, so that your child experiences increasing challenges.

The pages are designed for you to have fun with your child, or for the child to do independently and then share. A unique feature of the book is "For Grown-Ups," notes to help you support and extend your child's experience beyond the page.

Many of the activities have more than one "right" answer. Some ask your child to "look again." This open- ended approach allows children to work at their own level and to feel a sense of success. Keep it playful! Try the following activities for math play every day. Have fun, and remember, thinking <u>really is</u> child's play!

Ellen Booth Church

Ellen Booth Church

Math Every Day!

Children learn by doing. Here are simple activities to develop math concepts and skills in everyday life.

Sorting and Classifying

• Invite your child to help you sort and match socks, sort dark and light laundry, and put forks, spoons, and knives in their places in a drawer.

• Collect pebbles, seashells, or leaves and sort them. Guess how each of you sorted your items — by size, color, shape, or another characteristic. Name your groups. Then sort the same objects in a different way.

Patterns

• Find patterns everywhere you go! You'll see patterned tiles, fabrics, and even signs. As you and your child locate and describe patterns, you develop math language and concepts.

• Create patterns for one another to continue. Use everyday objects such as forks and spoons or colored beads in a simple a-b-a-b or a-b-c-a-b-c pattern, or draw and color patterns on paper. The possibilities are endless!

Shapes

• Look for shapes everywhere you go — circles and rectangles at the supermarket; triangles and rectangles in buildings and vehicles.

• Play shape games such as those on pp. 20-21 when you are waiting in a restaurant or doctor's office. All you need is paper and pencil! As you get better, you can set new tasks and rules.

Measuring and Comparing

• Use nonstandard measures to measure things for fun. "How many bananas tall are you?" "How many paper clips long is your toy boat?" "How many small bottles will fill this big one?"

• As you do everyday tasks with rulers and measuring cups, invite your child to help. Ask questions such as, "How many feet (rulers) wide is the window?" "How many cups are in a quart?"

It's Cleanup Time!

Where do the blocks go?
Draw lines to show.

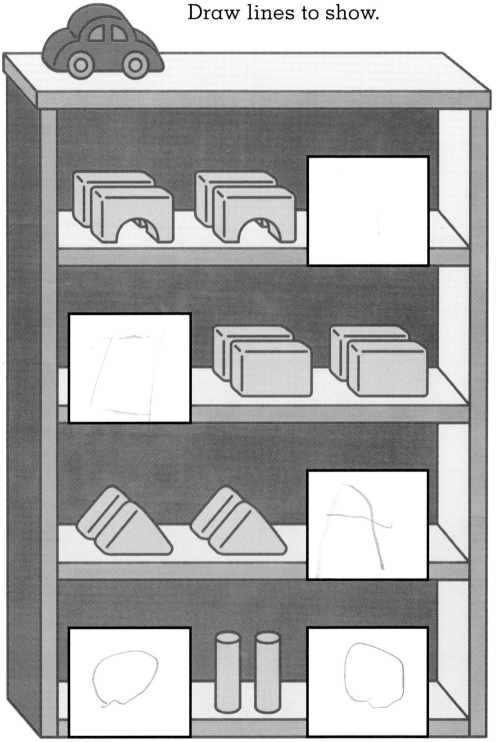
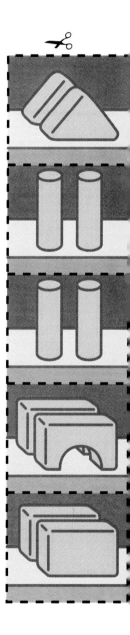

For Grown-Ups

Your child can differentiate and group items by pointing, drawing lines, or cutting and pasting the boxes where they belong. For more experience in classifying, play sorting games with buttons, blocks, or silverware.

Where Does It Go?

Help put things away.
Draw lines to show where things go.

For Grown-Ups

Discuss visual clues that suggest where each object belongs. Your child may sort by shapes
or by each item's function. Invite your child to help you clean up your own kitchen after meals.

Who Uses This?

Look at the pictures in the boxes.
Where does each thing go? Draw lines to show.

For Grown-Ups

Ask your child to identify each item and to explain what it is for. Point to a room and say, "What else might you find here?" Invite your child to talk about how the pictured school is the same as and different from his or her own school.

What Else Goes Here?

Draw something else that belongs on each line.

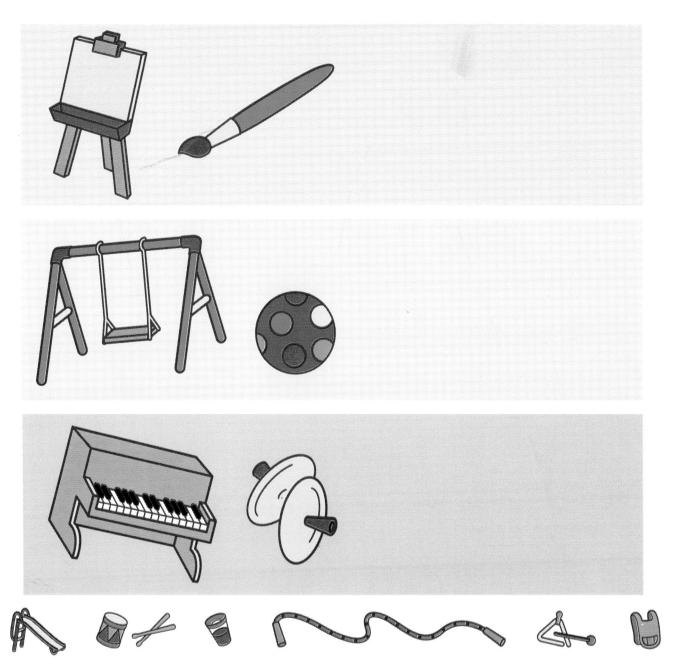

For Grown-Ups

Your child may come up with unexpected and creative ideas. Listen to the reasoning behind each choice. Play a game! Draw two objects that belong together, and ask your child to add one. Take turns drawing and guessing!

Fill in the Shapes!

What belongs in each box? Draw and color the shapes.

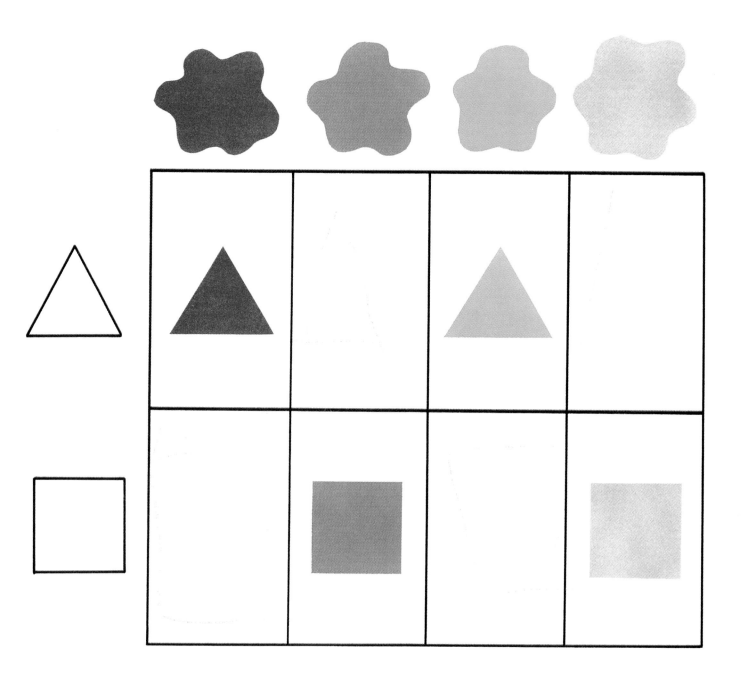

For Grown-Ups

This activity develops skill in classifying and logic. Talk about how your child knows what to draw in
the boxes, using questions like, "Would you put a blue circle here? Could we put a green triangle here?"

Fill in More Shapes!

What belongs in each box? Draw and color the shapes.

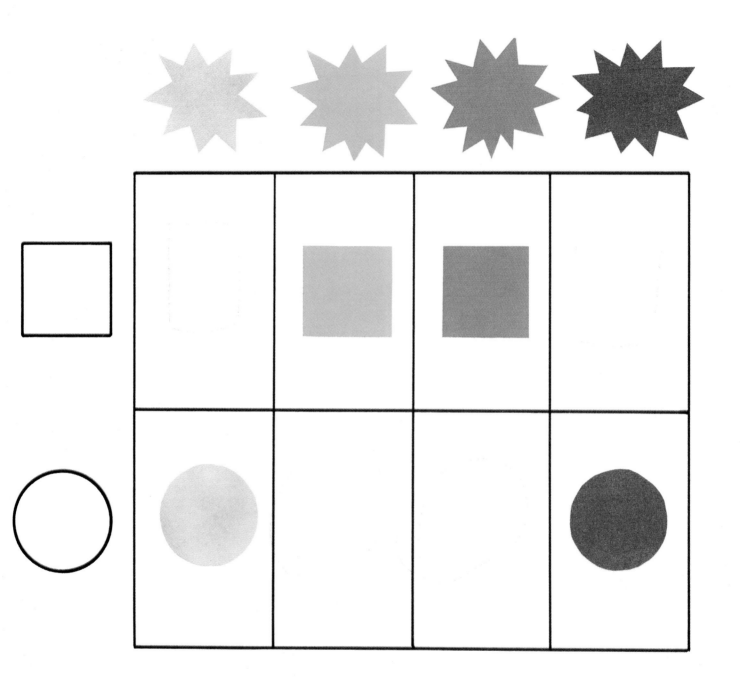

For Grown-Ups

Ask your child to identify the shapes and colors on the chart. Then add a diamond shape
and another row of boxes along the bottom of the chart. Invite your child to finish filling it in.

Look for Patterns

How many patterns do you see?
Use tally marks or numbers to count.

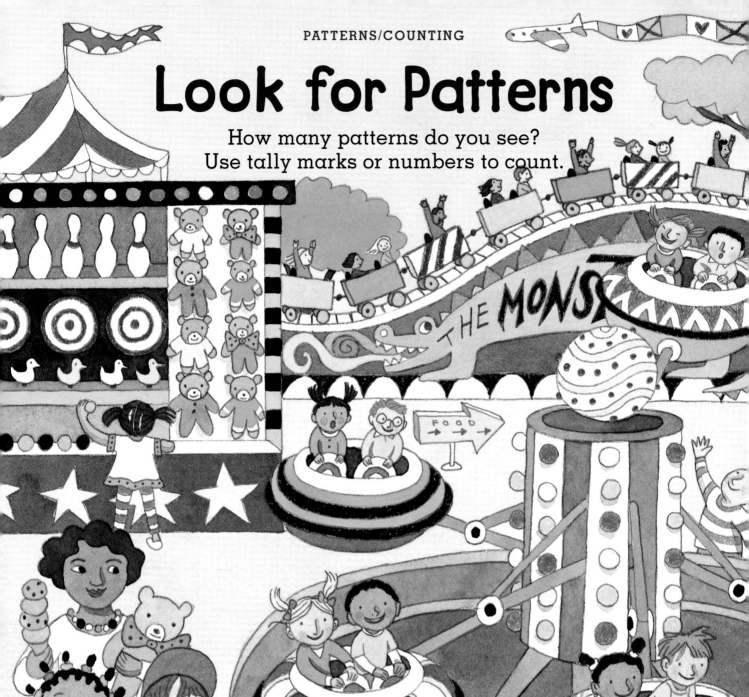

THE MONS

FOOD

Make a tally mark for each pattern

For Grown-Ups

Encourage your child to point out and describe each pattern. This is a "look again" activity because there are many patterns to find. Invite your child to look for patterns that are similar. Look for patterns in your home!

Find the Patterns

How many lizards have each pattern? Count.
Put tally marks or numbers in the boxes below.

For Grown-Ups

For more counting, ask how many lizards, tails, feet, and eyes are on the page. Count them together.
Have fun drawing lizards, turtles, and other animals with bright patterns!

11

Finish the Patterns!

What comes next? Finish the patterns. Color or draw.

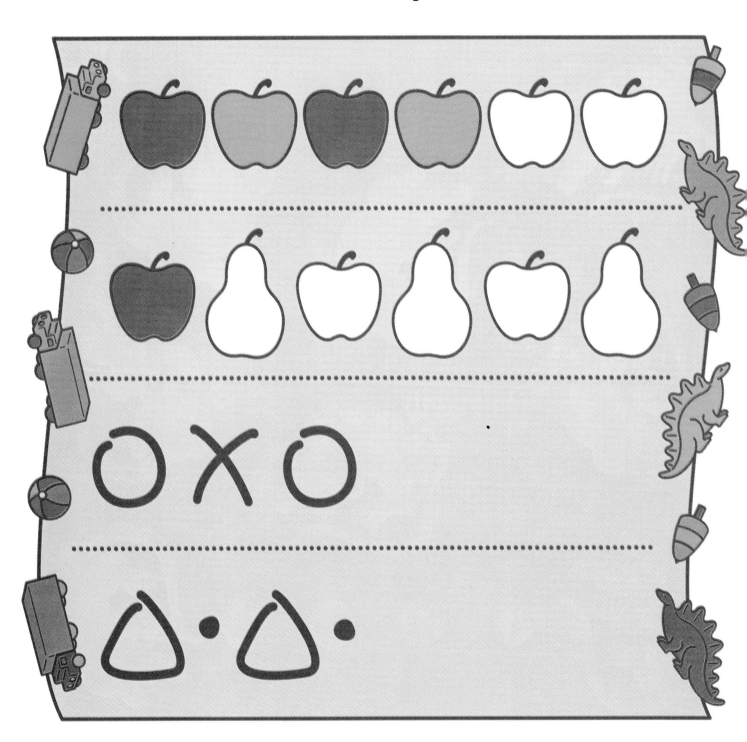

For Grown-Ups

Ask your child to tell you about his or her pattern choices. Make up and draw other patterns together. You can also make patterns with real fruits and vegetables or household objects such as forks and spoons or socks and shoes.

Slithery Snakes

Color the patterns. Make your own pattern on the middle snake.

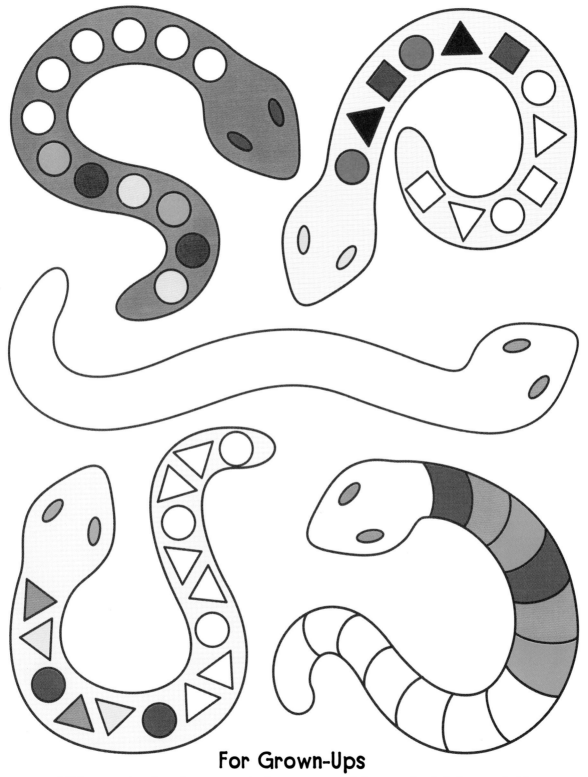

For Grown-Ups

Does your child recognize that the pattern is the same on all four snakes? Ask your child to identify what is creating the pattern on each snake (shapes or color) before he or she colors the middle snake.

15

What Shape Is It?

Look for the shapes. How many of each?

△ _____ □ _____ ○ _____ ▢ _____

For Grown-Ups

Talk about the buildings and how the shapes are used in them. For example, roofs can be made of triangles, and windows can be made of circles, rectangles, or squares. Do a shape hunt outside. How many of each shape do you find

What Do You See?

Look for shapes. How many of each?

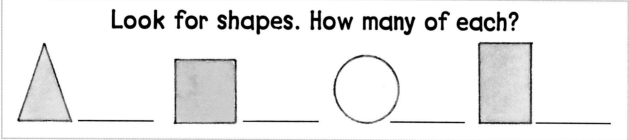

For Grown-Ups

Your child may include plates as circles or menus as rectangles as he or she counts shapes. Some of the items pictured are not drawn from a head-on perspective, but your child may use prior knowledge to identify their shapes.

17

Look for Shapes

How many of each shape?

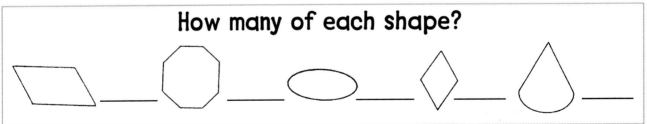

For Grown-Ups

Which shapes were easiest to find? Which were hardest? Are there any shapes in the picture that are not on the chart?
Think of names for the rides and buildings together. Draw different-shaped signs to label each one.

18

Color the Shapes

How many of each?

△ _____ □ _____ ▭ _____

For Grown-Ups

Ask your child to tell you about the boats and their different parts. Help your child draw similar shapes, color them, and cut them out. Use them to create new objects — your own puzzle!

Draw Squares

Draw lines to connect the dots.
Make big and little squares!

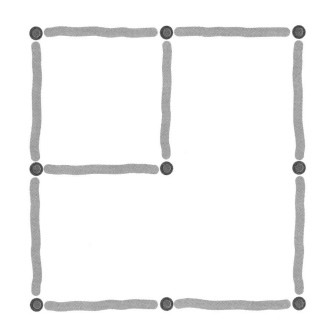

How many did you make? _____

For Grown-Ups

Help your child see that there can be little squares inside a big square. Find big and little squares that make up things in your home, such as floor or wall tiles, windows, or framed pictures.

Draw Triangles

Draw lines to connect the dots.
Make as many triangles as you can.

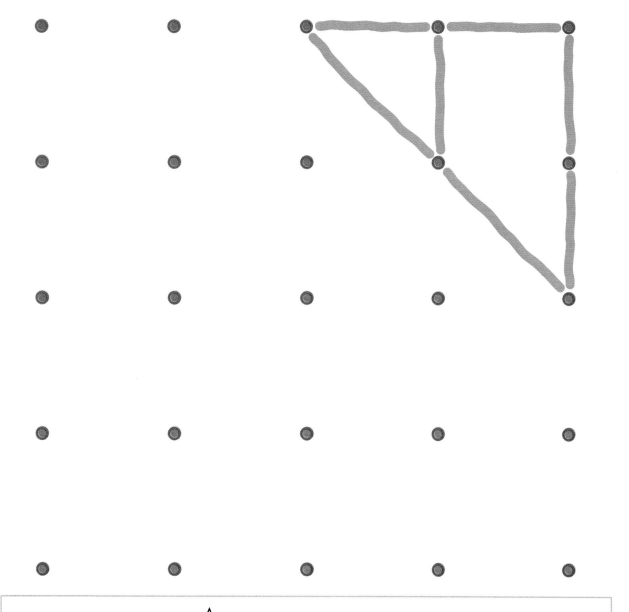

How many  did you make? _____

For Grown-Ups

With your child's help, make another grid of five dots across and five dots down. Take turns
drawing triangles until the grid is all filled up. How many triangles did you and your child draw?

Are You My Mother?

Match the puppies to their mothers.
Draw lines. Draw your own mother and puppy.

How many mothers? ———

How many puppies? ———

For Grown-Ups

Provide additional paper for your child's drawing if it is needed. Invite your child to tell a story about the mother dog and puppy he or she drew. Encourage use of the words *big* and *little*.

22

Longer and Shorter

How many worms are longer than  ? ⬜

How many insects are shorter than  ? ⬜

Circle the longest snail.

Circle something that is longer than any worm.

For Grown-Ups

Invite your child to show you which animals are longer or shorter than the striped beetle.
Use household objects such as buttons or pieces of string to measure the worms, snails, and insects.

How Long Is It?

Use pennies to measure.
Write the number or use tally marks.

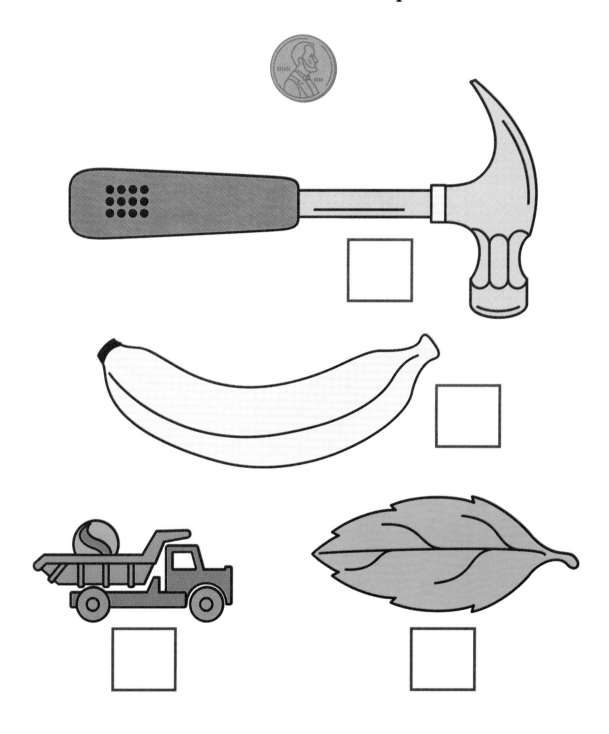

For Grown-Ups

Encourage your child to show you how she or he used a real penny to measure one of
the items on the page. Then let your child use pennies to measure real household objects.

Use a Ruler!

Cut out the ruler.
Use it to measure.

inches
1
2
3
4
5
6

How many inches?

✿		✎	
◯		◗	
◖		🌀	
🍃		🐢	

For Grown-Ups

Talk about each natural object. Make comparative statements, such as "The turtle is 1 inch longer than the shell." Use the ruler to measure household objects or things you find on a nature walk.

Park the Vehicles

Measure the vehicles with a penny, paper clip, or ruler. Measure the parking spaces. Cut and paste.

For Grown-Ups

Ask your child to demonstrate measuring one of the vehicles. Together, draw a city block lined with different-sized parking spaces. Use toy cars and trucks to fill some of the spaces.

PARK HERE

27

Let's Play Cards!

Cut out the cards. Use them to play games.
Make up your own card games!

Sort It Out

Mix up the cards.
How many ways can you sort them?

Make Patterns

Try shape patterns.
Try size patterns.
What other patterns can you make?

The Memory Game

Spread out the cards face down.
Choose two cards.
Did you make a match?
If not, turn the cards over.
Keep trying until all the cards are matched.

For Grown-Ups

Help your child cut out the cards. Play games together. Talk about which
game you liked best, and ask your child which game is his or her favorite.
Make up your own game!

Tic-Tac-Toe!

Cut out the shapes.
Use them to play tic-tac-toe!

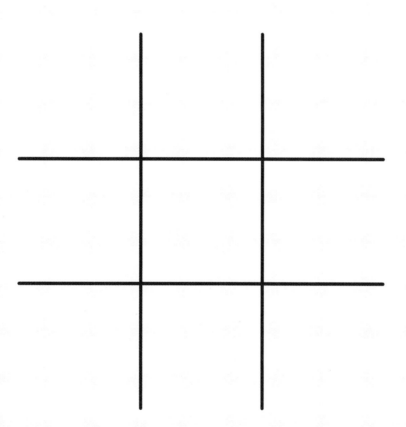

For Grown-Ups

With your child, make a three-dimensional tic-tac-toe game with round and square objects. For instance, make a tabletop game using napkins and plates, or a game on a bed with pillows and beanbags!

31

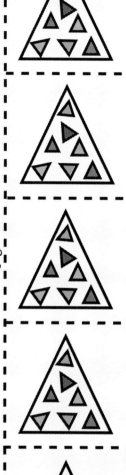

Tic-Tac-Toe!

Cut out the shapes!
Use them to play tic-tac-toe!

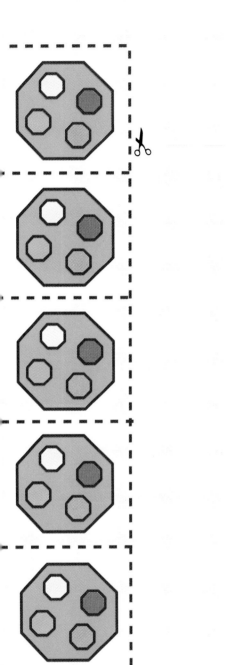

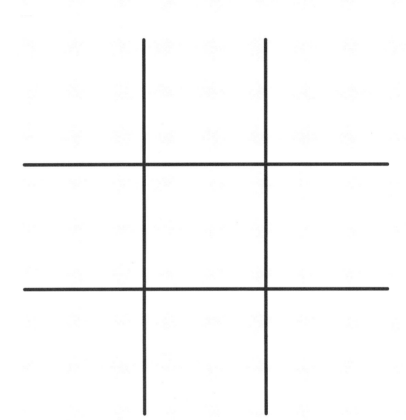

For Grown-Ups
Invite your child to use shapes to make patterns without the grid. Play a "Guess My Pattern" game — take turns guessing and continuing each other's patterns.

32

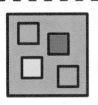
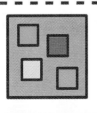
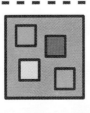
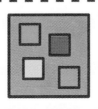
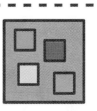